Quick! Make sure you write your name in this book! Otherwise a ten-headed dude might steal it!

_____

NAME

– – – – – – – – – – – – – –

– – – – – – – – – – – – – –

GHEE HAPPY

HEY! This book belongs to me RAVANA.

GHEE HAPPY BOOKSHELF

Ganesha's **Great Race**

Ganesha's **Sweet Tooth**

Ghee Happy Gods & Goddesses: A Little Board Book of Hindu Deities

Ramayana: Divine Loophole

The Little Book of **Hindu Deities**

The Big Poster Book of Hindu Deities

The Art of **Sanjay's Super Team**

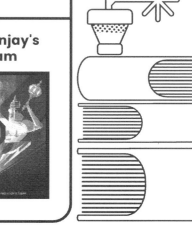

Diwali
COLORING BOOK

GHEE HAPPY
STUDIO

Library of Congress Cataloging-in-Publication Data is
available

ISBN: 979-8-3404-7850-4

Made in the USA Las Vegas, NV

Art by the Ghee Happy Art & Design team:
Chris Ohara, Ryan Matias, David Maingault, & Sanjay Patel
Typeface Poppins Designed by Jonny Pinhorn & Ninad Kale
Typeface Big Softie by HouseOfBurvo

10 9 8 7 6 5 4 3 2 1

Ghee Happy Studio Inc.
18 Dharma Drive
North Hollywood, CA 91601
www.gheehappy.com

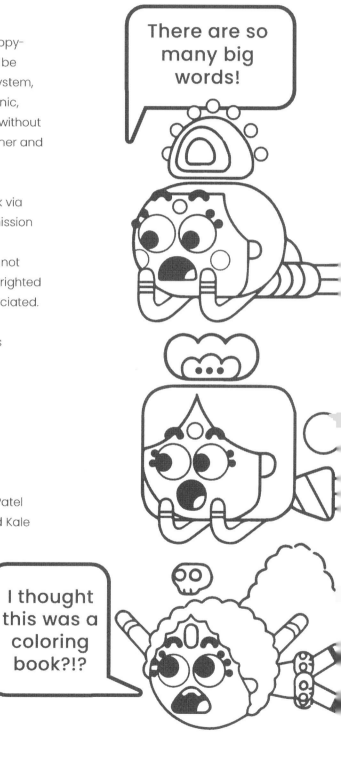

TABLE OF CONTENTS

What is Diwali?

Diwali, also called Deepavali, is a fun and special holiday celebrated by millions of people around the world. It's known as the **Festival of Lights** because people decorate their homes with lots of beautiful lights and tiny lamps called diyas.

People also light fireworks and make yummy sweets, and share gifts to welcome happiness and good luck into their lives. It's a way of celebrating love, kindness, and all the good things in life!

Ghee Gods

Meet the four great Hindu deities, **Ganesha**, **Kali**, **Krishna**, and **Saraswati,** (aka **Swati**) reimagined as kids! The adorable little Ghee Gods attend a school called Ghee Happy and are guided by a monk with a big heart and a small vocabulary named **Guru.**

Ganesha

The little God of beginnings

Swati

The little Goddess of knowledge

Krishna | The little God of play

Kali | The little Goddess of destruction

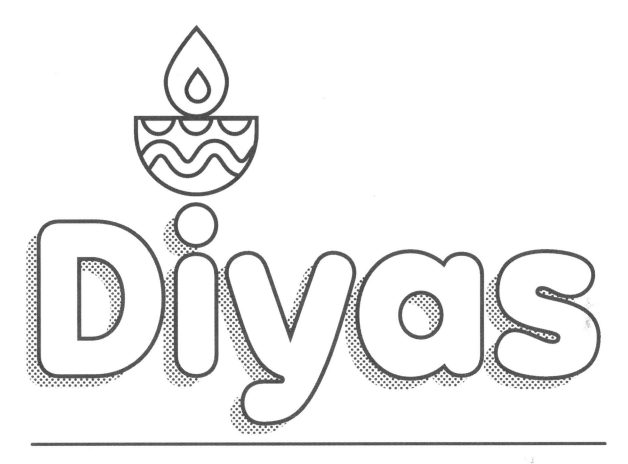

Diyas

A diya is like a tiny, beautiful lamp that helps bring light to the world during Diwali! People light these little lamps to celebrate happiness, love, and the victory of good over bad. The light from the diya also helps welcome friends, family, and even the goddess Lakshmi, who brings luck and good fortune. When you light a diya, it's like you're spreading brightness and joy all around!

Diwali lanterns are colorful decorations
that people hang outside their homes
during the festival of Diwali.

Fireworks

During Diwali, fireworks and sparklers are used to celebrate the festival and make the night sky bright and colorful.

Rangoli

Rangolis are colorful patterns made on the ground during Diwali using materials like colored powders, chalk, and flower petals.

Offering **sweets,** also known as *mithai,* during Diwali is a way to spread happiness, joy, and good wishes for the new year.

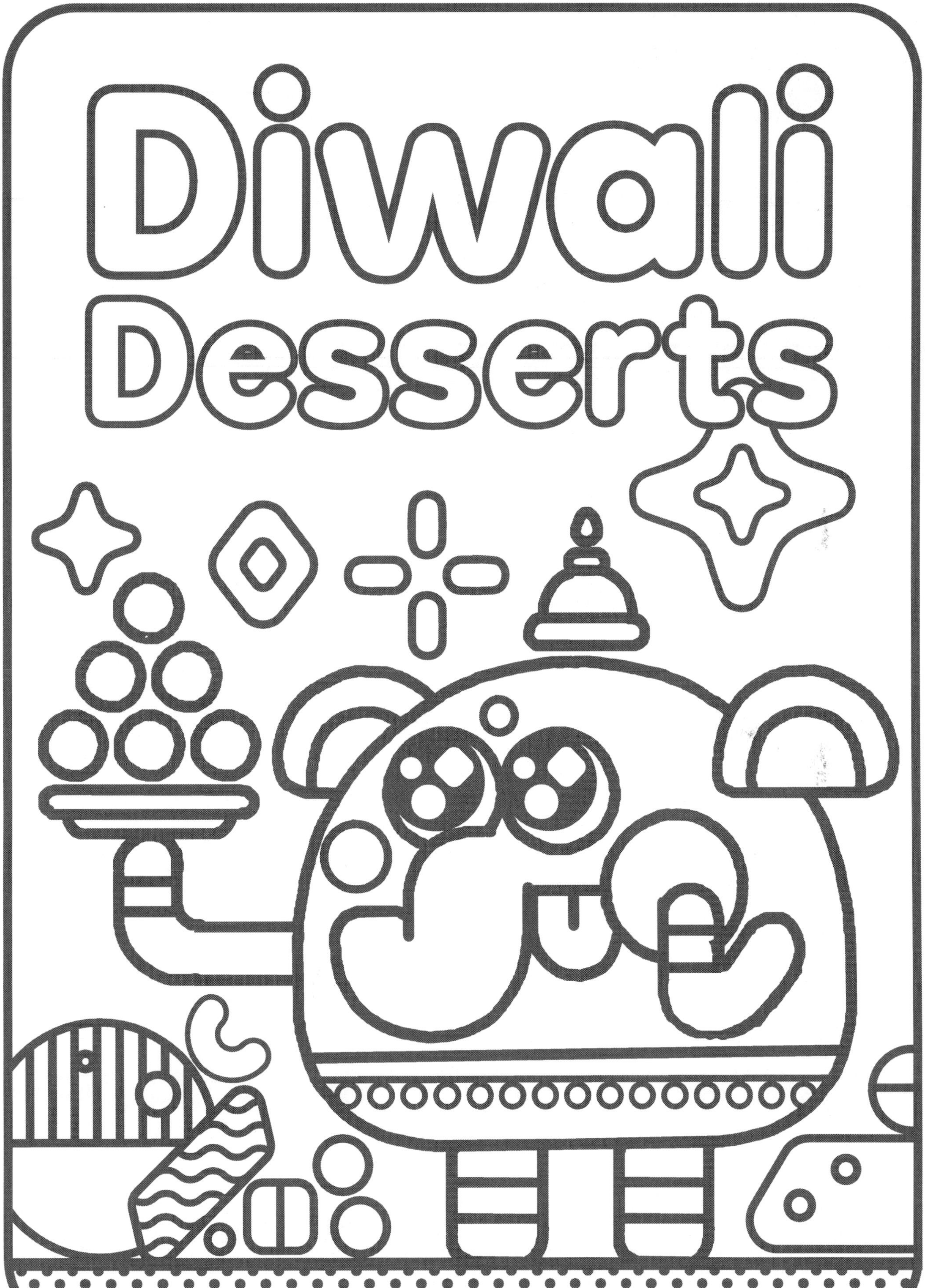
Diwali Desserts

Don't forget to enjoy some healthy
snacks this Diwali, too!

Goddess Lakshmi

During Diwali, many people believe that **Lakshmi**, the goddess of wealth and prosperity, visits their homes to give blessings. She brings good fortune, happiness, and success.

During Diwali, rows of lamps are placed in doorways, windows, and around the house to guide **Lakshmi** inside.

Music

Music and dancing often happen at Diwali parties and community events, making the celebration even more fun and lively!

Diwali is not just about prayers and lights—it's also a time filled with fun, laughter, and joy! Families get together, share jokes, and have a great time.

Why did the lamp go to school on Diwali?

Because it wanted to be a little brighter!

HAVE A BALL THIS DIWALI

What do you call a Diwali celebration for birds?

A "super fly" festival!

What's better than Diwali?
TEN HEADS!

Hey, Ghee Happy friends! It's me, **Sanjay Patel**, the Ghee goofball himself. I hope you're enjoying the coloring book so far. Most of the artwork was created by the amazing Ghee Happy artists behind the animated series. If you like what you see here, you'll love the show—check it out on YouTube!

Before you go, I wanted to also share a short comic that I made, inspired by my boys, *Arjun and Kiran*. I hope it tickles your funny bone and inspires a joyful Diwali for you and your family.

This comic is also for coloring! So keep going with your creations and once you're done send me a photo at **gheehappystudio@gmail.com**

-Sanjay

THE **SUPER SILLY**

Adventures of Rule-Following
RAMA and Rude **RAVANA**

with Extra FUN and LAUGHS for Kiran & Arjun!!!

*To parents and old folks, this is meant to be silly, so if this makes you grumpy
please find your nearest whoopie cushion and sit on it.*

DIWALI DUEL!

By Sanjay Patel

Of course there's MORE!
LOTS MORE!!

Learn all about why Ravana flushed nine of his heads in the toilet!!!

I'll **RUIN** Rama's plumbing!!!!!!!

Skibidi Toilet!

Discover why Sita writes Mother's Day cards to the dirt!

HINT Sita was born from the ground!

Dear Mother Earth,

I dig you cause your the dirtiest Mom a daughter could ever have!

Sita

And of course go on awesome adventures with Hanuman!!!!

cause let's face it, Hanuman might be cooler than Hulk, Thor, and Superman all rolled into one.

Dosen't get better than a flying monkey!

All that and more in the next issue!!

the Return of RAVANA & his Rude-Talkin' Root Beer!!!

Every bubble is loaded with RUDE talkin' burps!

Your breath STINKS!

Butt brain!

You only have ONE dumb head!

USE THIS SPECIAL CODE TO UNLOCK THE NEXT ISSUE.

Made in the USA
Las Vegas, NV
20 October 2024

10066257R00065